The British Museum

FIND TOM IN TIME

Michelangelo's Italy

About Michelangelo's Italy

Michelangelo was born in 1475 and spent much of his life as an artist in Florence, Italy. Michelangelo lived in Florence during a time known as the *Renaissance*, a period of time over 500 years ago when people believed in bringing new ideas to art, business and politics, as well as continuing existing religious beliefs. Florence was a rich city that celebrated artists, so it was a perfect place for Michelangelo to grow up. As well as being known for its art, the people of Florence loved throwing sporting events, festivals and parties, including grand balls! Some of the places that Tom visits in this book may not have existed together at the same time, but they were all part of Renaissance Florence's culture and history.

Get ready to meet . . .

Tom

Granny Bea

Digby the cat

and spot the hidden Medici coat of arms in every scene!

First published 2022

Nosy Crow Ltd
The Crow's Nest, 14 Baden Place,
Crosby Row, London, SE1 1YW, UK

Nosy Crow Eireann Ltd
44 Orchard Grove, Kenmare,
Co Kerry, V93 FY22, Ireland

www.nosycrow.com

ISBN 978 1 83994 215 0 (HB)
ISBN 978 1 83994 216 7 (PB)

Nosy Crow and associated logos are trademarks
and/or registered trademarks of Nosy Crow Ltd.
Published in collaboration with the British Museum.

Text © Nosy Crow 2022
Illustrations © Fatti Burke 2022

The right of Nosy Crow to be identified as the author and Fatti Burke
to be identified as the illustrator of this work has been asserted.
A CIP catalogue record for this book is available from the British Library.

Printed in China.
Papers used by Nosy Crow are made from wood
grown in sustainable forests.

1 3 5 7 9 8 6 4 2
1 3 5 7 9 8 6 4 2

Contents

INTRODUCTION

Tom was an ordinary boy, most of the time.
He was clever and brave, and he loved adventure.

Tom's grandmother, Bea, was an ordinary grandmother, most of the time. She was clever and brave, and a little bit mischievous, and she loved adventure, too. Which was just as well, since her job was digging in the dust and the dirt to discover how people used to live. Granny Bea was an **ARCHAEOLOGIST**.

Granny Bea's cat, Digby, did not like digging in the dust and the dirt. Or getting wet. Or missing his meals. In fact, Digby did not like adventure at all. Especially after what happened the last time Tom came to stay . . . but that's another story.

One warm, sunny day Granny Bea called Tom up to her study. Digby was sitting on her lap while she inspected something carefully in the sunlight.

"What's that?" asked Tom, staring at something glinting in her hand.

Granny Bea grinned, holding out her palm. "It's a hat badge from the time of Michelangelo. He was a famous Italian artist who lived more than 500 years ago, during a time called the Renaissance. In Florence, where he grew up, the people wore beautiful clothing and jewellery."

Tom reached out slowly to touch the hat badge and . . . *WHOOSH!*

MEDICI SCULPTURE GARDEN

Tom was in Renaissance Florence. This was incredible! He was in some sort of garden, filled with green hedges, flowers and many sculptures.

All around, people were reading, enjoying the plants or studying the art. But where was Granny Bea? Suddenly, Tom saw a flash of orange move towards the street. Digby!

The garden belonged to the rich **MEDICI** family, and was originally designed to display their large collection of Roman sculpture. People during the Renaissance tried to learn from how the ancient Romans taught, wrote, created art and thought about the world. They thought that everyone should have knowledge of as wide a range of topics as possible.

The people of Florence believed that creating architecture and art brought them closer to God. Artists became very important in Renaissance society because they could make the city more beautiful.

CAN YOU SPOT?

- Tom
- A group of artists sketching a sculpture
- A gardener carrying a tree
- Digby the cat
- Children playing a game of chess
- A statue that has lost its head
- A stonemason moving some marble

The sculpture garden was a place where artists could come to study and sketch, and there was even a nearby villa where the Medici family allowed some artists to stay while they worked. Solid marble and stone from the garden were also moved and then worked on by **STONEMASONS** in other parts of the city, including in the home of Lorenzo de' Medici, the head of the Medici family.

PIAZZA DeLLa SIGNORIA

Tom raced out of the garden and down narrow streets until he reached a busy square. All of the people there were wearing tunics or dresses.

Turning around, he realised that a child behind him was offering him a tunic of his own! Thanking the child, Tom pulled it on over his clothes and made his way through the square, searching for Digby as he went.

The Piazza della Signoria was the square where the government, or **SIGNORIA**, met. As it was where decisions were made, the square itself became the main place for people to meet and swap gossip or to make secret political plans.

The **FLORENTINE** people were afraid of one group or family becoming too powerful, so they created a system where everyone in the government would be swapped out for someone new every two months. Names would be picked out of bags to choose new officials.

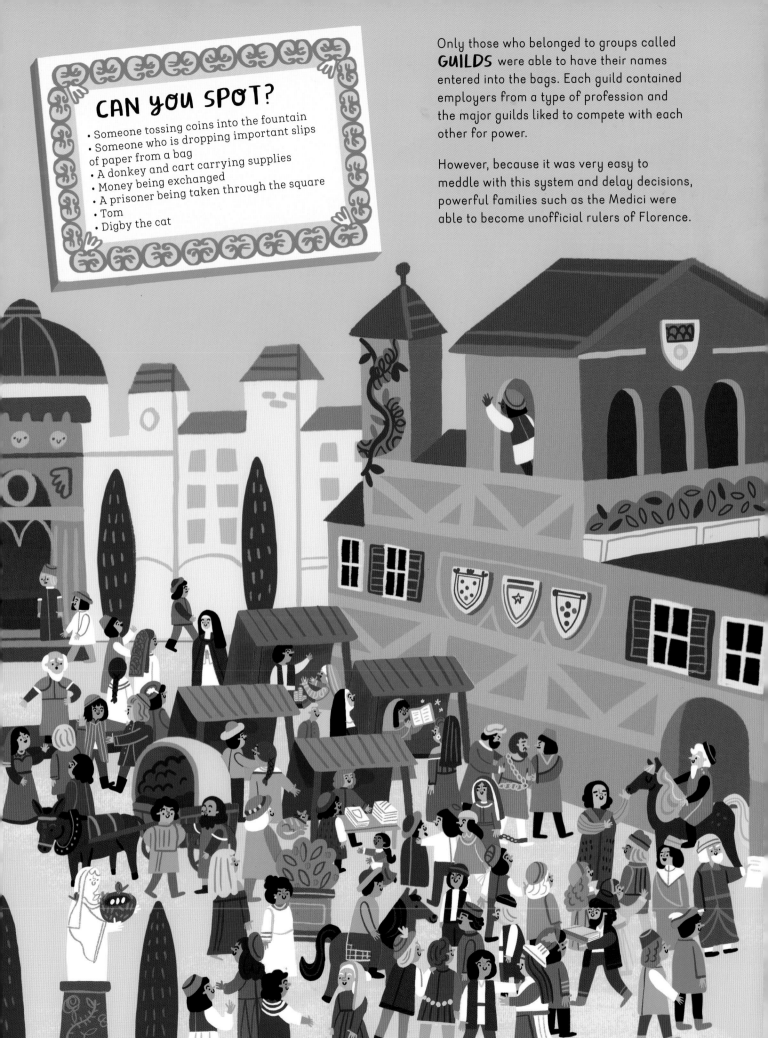

CAN YOU SPOT?

- Someone tossing coins into the fountain
- Someone who is dropping important slips of paper from a bag
- A donkey and cart carrying supplies
- Money being exchanged
- A prisoner being taken through the square
- Tom
- Digby the cat

Only those who belonged to groups called **GUILDS** were able to have their names entered into the bags. Each guild contained employers from a type of profession and the major guilds liked to compete with each other for power.

However, because it was very easy to meddle with this system and delay decisions, powerful families such as the Medici were able to become unofficial rulers of Florence.

WEDDING PROCESSION

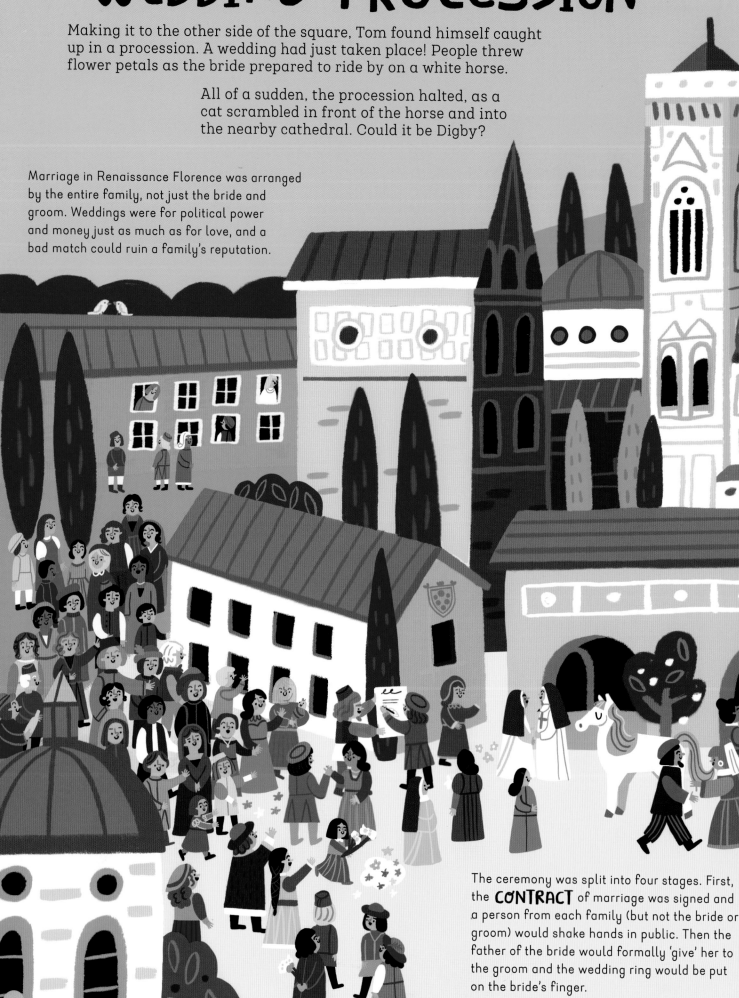

Making it to the other side of the square, Tom found himself caught up in a procession. A wedding had just taken place! People threw flower petals as the bride prepared to ride by on a white horse.

All of a sudden, the procession halted, as a cat scrambled in front of the horse and into the nearby cathedral. Could it be Digby?

Marriage in Renaissance Florence was arranged by the entire family, not just the bride and groom. Weddings were for political power and money just as much as for love, and a bad match could ruin a family's reputation.

The ceremony was split into four stages. First, the **CONTRACT** of marriage was signed and a person from each family (but not the bride or groom) would shake hands in public. Then the father of the bride would formally 'give' her to the groom and the wedding ring would be put on the bride's finger.

CAN YOU SPOT?

- A woman with a baby
- The bride's wedding chest
- Tom
- An elderly couple dancing together
- Digby the cat
- A group of musicians
- A contract of marriage

Next would be a large celebration in the form of a procession or feast, and finally a serious religious ceremony. The bride would wear a silk or satin gown and her wedding chest, called a **CASSONE**, would be carried with her through the streets. The cassone held all of her possessions and would sometimes be painted with scenes of a wedding feast.

Women whose families could not afford marriages were sometimes sent to **CONVENTS** to become nuns!

FLORENCE CATHEDRAL

Tom entered the doors of the cathedral, but there was no sign of Digby. He walked across the patterned floor and gasped as he found himself standing under a huge dome, beautifully painted by men on high scaffolding.

Looking back down, Tom spotted a familiar-looking old lady leaving the cathedral . . .

The many guilds of Florence liked to show off how important they were by becoming **PATRONS** of different buildings across the city. They would try to make their chosen building more stunning and famous than any other by hosting competitions for artists to come up with special designs for their projects.

The **WOOL GUILD** was one of the most influential guilds in the city because so many people worked in that industry. Florence Cathedral was completed after the guild held a competition to design the dome. Before this competition was held, the cathedral remained unfinished for 80 years!

As well as being a place for people to pray, the inside of the cathedral was covered in pieces of sculpture and paintings for people to admire. It was also a place where teenagers could meet to gossip.

CAN YOU SPOT?

- An artist painting upside down
- A group of teenagers chatting on a bench
- Tom
- A group of women praying
- A table covered in wool
- Someone about to light a candle
- Digby the cat

MICHELANGELO'S STUDIO

Back in the street, Tom followed the old lady to the door of a simple building. Inside, he found a sculptor hard at work. It was Michelangelo!

The old lady had vanished, but an orange tail flicked around the corner of a sculpture by the doorway. "Digby!" Tom called out.

Michelangelo's talent led to him becoming one of the most influential artists in Italy. His paintings and poems were very well known, but Michelangelo's real passion was **SCULPTURE**.

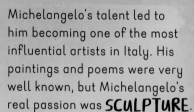

He started work as an **APPRENTICE** to a painter, but he also spent time sketching in the Medici sculpture garden, trying to copy the style of the sculptures there. Michelangelo carved in marble, with the idea that it was his job to free a hidden piece of art from within the rock rather than to create it from scratch.

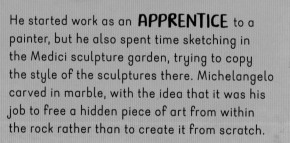

CAN YOU SPOT?

- Michelangelo working on a sculpture on a ladder
- A woman reading a book of poetry
- An orange sculpture that looks just like Digby
- Tom
- Carving tools on a table
- A painting of the Medici sculpture garden
- Digby the cat

One of his most famous marble sculptures, **DAVID**, was designed for one of Florence's central town squares and was loved by the people of the city. Michelangelo worked for over 70 years and was never afraid to give his honest opinion to other artists of the Renaissance. He inspired a painting style called **MANNERISM**, where artists decided to paint figures and objects less realistically and in more exaggerated poses in order to create the painting that they wanted.

PONTE VeCCHIO

Tom raced after Digby, but the naughty cat vanished just as they reached a stone bridge, stretching over a wide river.

Shops selling colourful goods were crammed all the way across the bridge and people were buying all kinds of wonderful things. Where had Digby got to?

Ponte Vecchio means 'old bridge' in Italian. It was built during the **MEDIEVAL** period and by the time of the Renaissance had been standing for hundreds of years. Shops were built all the way along the bridge and were originally occupied by fishmongers and butchers.

CAN YOU SPOT?

- Digby the cat
- Someone pouring out water and waste
- A fishmonger selling a bucket of fish
- Tom
- A woman selling tomatoes
- A donkey munching on some hay
- A dog stealing some meat

Wasted scraps of food, fish guts and animal bones could be easily thrown into the **ARNO RIVER** below, but the constant selling of raw fish and meat meant that the bridge was very noisy and smelly! Eventually, it was decided that jewellers and other non-food **MERCHANTS** would take over the shops on the bridge while the original merchants moved elsewhere.

The rich and important Medici family of Florence wanted to be able to cross the bridge without having to mix with the commoners in the marketplace. They ordered a special **PASSAGEWAY** to be built above the shops on the Ponte Vecchio so that they could cross the river in peace and privacy.

THE ARNO RIVER

Crossing the bridge, Tom made his way along the side of the river. There were boats unloading all around him and it seemed that he saw wool everywhere he looked!

A group of children began to laugh and Tom saw a wool-covered, cat-shaped creature dart towards the city gates.

Florence was built on the banks of the river Arno, which connected the city with the sea 80 kilometres away. Access to the river meant that it was easy to transport materials to the city to be worked with and then **TRADED** on. Florence became very important in the trade of wool and many of the Florentine people had jobs turning freshly sheared **RAW WOOL** into finished cloth for sale.

Masses of raw wool from across Europe would be unloaded from boats along the river and collected into piles. Then it would be washed in the river before being sorted by quality. Finally, it would be hung up to dry before being taken away to be dyed, combed, spun and woven.

CAN YOU SPOT?

- Two children playing with dolls
- Tom
- A young boy collecting scraps of wool
- Dyed cloth being hung in a shed
- Digby the cat
- Someone who has fallen asleep in a pile of wool
- A boat with a leak

Finished cloth would be stretched and dried in sheds by the river, before it was collected by boat and transported out of Florence to be sold for expensive clothing. The city made a lot of its wealth from using the river Arno and became famous for its high-quality goods.

COUNTRYSIDE

Exiting the walls of the city, Tom followed dusty paw prints to a beautiful vineyard, surrounded by hills and villas. A crowd had gathered around a man with a strange-looking machine.

As the man was preparing to test his invention, Tom heard a distant meow. He headed in the direction of the sound.

The hills around Florence were filled with farms and **VILLAS**. Rich families used the villas that they built as an escape from the city, but they also hired farmers to take care of their land. In the late summer, workers collected olives from trees, **PLOUGHED** fields, and **PRUNED** vines to use the grapes to make wine. When the harvest was bad, farm workers moved to the city centre to find new jobs.

CAN YOU SPOT?

- Leonardo's flying machine
- A farmer who is taking a nap
- Tom
- Leonardo doing a sketch
- A man sneakily eating some olives
- A donkey with an empty cart
- Digby the cat

The countryside was not just for rich merchants and farmers – famous artists such as **LEONARDO DA VINCI** would come to the countryside to draw and build. Leonardo enjoyed sketching horses and would sit in the hills, observing them for hours.

Although he is most famous for his paintings, such as the **MONA LISA**, Leonardo da Vinci was also an inventor. He designed and attempted to make some early versions of objects that are used today, including parachutes and life jackets. The hills outside of Florence acted as a good testing place for some of these inventions, including a **FLYING MACHINE**!

COMBAT TRAINING

Tom turned a corner – and came face to face with an army!
A group of soldiers on horseback were training together. All of the horses wore decorative coats and the men wore smart uniforms.

From behind the horses, Tom caught sight of Digby . . .
being carried away in the arms of a soldier.

Italian towns and cities were often at war with other local areas, and Florence was no different. Originally, boys and men aged between 15 and 70 were recruited by local leaders to fight for their city. However, the townspeople were eventually replaced with professionally trained fighters, called **MERCENARIES**, who would defend Florence for money.

The leader of the mercenary army was called a **CONDOTTIERE**, and they commanded the loyalty of the other soldiers who were paid to fight. A condottiere would sign a contract with the city or town that he defended, and this would control how many men the city could hire and how much money the soldiers would make.

CAN YOU SPOT?

- Tom
- A knight whose armour is too heavy
- A condottiere signing his contract
- Digby the cat
- A crossbow that has misfired
- A child who has snuck on to a horse
- A soldier with dirty armour

As well as using traditional **KNIGHTS** on horseback with swords, the mercenary army in Florence also had **CROSSBOWS** and guns, and **CANNONS** that could be fired from the city walls.

Men who fought in lighter armour defended the knights, to stop them from being removed from their horses. At this time, a knight's armour was so heavy that if they fell, they would not be able to get up again!

Festival Games

Tom hurriedly followed the soldier back towards the city, but lost sight of him as they turned into a square. A sporting event was taking place and children in the crowd were waving banners and cheering for their team!

Catching his breath, Tom heard a surprised yowl and gasped as he saw Digby jump out of the way of a ball and flee down an alley.

CALCIO was an early version of football and was a very popular sport in Florence. During festivals, a square in the city would be covered in sand and split into two halves, to become a playing field with a goal running across the width of the square at each end. Each team would be made up of 27 players, including four **DATORI INDIETRO** or goalies.

A calcio match would last for 50 minutes, starting with a cannon blast. Each team would try and use the ball to score as many goals, or **CACCE**, as possible in the time given. Players were allowed to use their bodies to try and stop the other team, and matches could become very violent. If a player was injured, they had to either quit or keep going – no replacement players were allowed for either team.

CAN YOU SPOT?

- The referee shouting angrily
- An athlete who is covered in sand
- Tom
- A player who has fallen over
- Digby the cat
- The cannon used to start the match
- A rat that has snuck on to the playing field

A modern version of calcio is still played today! While teams in the Renaissance would have been awarded a pure-bred cow as a prize, today's winning team are instead offered a free dinner at a restaurant.

ARTIST WORKSHOP

Heading down the alley, Tom spotted Digby climbing through the window of a nearby building.

Creeping inside, he saw a group of artists painting, sketching with charcoal and decorating furniture.

A sudden crash made everyone look up – Digby had knocked over a jar of paint! The clumsy cat padded out of the room, leaving a trail of painted paw prints behind him.

As well as hiring famous painters and sculptors like Michelangelo, whose works were precious and very expensive, people could also purchase smaller and cheaper works of art from hundreds of other artists who had workshops in Florence.

Florentines would buy art for different reasons. Paintings could be used as religious objects and paintings of the **MADONNA**, or Virgin Mary, were often copied and sold for low prices. A painting or an object, such as a cassone, could be **COMMISSIONED** to celebrate a special occasion like a wedding. Some very rich people might even pay for a work of art that would take years to create, so that they could become the owners of a masterpiece.

CAN YOU SPOT?

- Two people mixing different paint colours
- Someone getting measured for a new outfit
- An artist painting some furniture
- A family having their portrait painted
- Digby the cat
- Tom
- An artist creating copies of a painting

Workshops could have many artists working in them at one time. They often made their own paints and charcoal, and could work with cloth, sketch, paint or sculpt. Some workshops made one specific type of item and others produced many types of art made by different artists.

PALAZZO MEDICI

Tom tracked the painted paw prints until they ended just inside the open door of a grand building. Tiptoeing carefully, he made his way towards a dining room, where a feast was taking place.

The food smelled amazing! Digby was always hungry – he must be somewhere close by.

The **SALA** was the biggest room in the home and was used for both entertaining and dining. While poorer families mainly ate meals of bread and vegetables, many ordinary Florentines could afford to eat meat around once a week, and wealthy families might enjoy pigeon, veal, or chicken dishes regularly. During a feast to celebrate a wedding or a holy day, special or unusual meals would be served – such as a pie with live blackbirds hiding inside it!

While forks had been invented, they were mainly used to serve individual portions from a larger plate. People did have knives and crockery, but they mostly ate with their hands. Husbands and wives would also share the same plate.

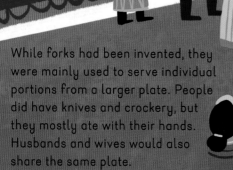

CAN YOU SPOT?

- Tom
- A husband and wife sharing a plate of vegetables
- A hungry dog
- Digby the cat
- A blackbird pie
- A spilled flask of wine
- A servant dropping some meat

The church of Florence taught that it was important to give to others. Townspeople could form a **CONFRATERNITY** and use this group to give leftover food to very poor Florentines. This leftover food would be much simpler than that eaten by the rich, and a weekly allowance could be as little as a flask of wine and three loaves of bread.

CARNIVAL BALL

Tom heard a satisfied meow and headed towards the sound.
In the courtyard of the building a ball was taking place!
Men and woman in ornate clothing danced to music, while
overhead fireworks were released into the evening sky.

Just then, Tom glimpsed Digby, happily eating a piece of
chicken. He was sitting in the arms of . . . Granny Bea!

Florence had feasts and festivals
all year round, but the summertime
was the perfect setting for some
of their biggest celebrations. As
well as outdoor calcio games,
there would also be parades of
crafted scenery, and evening balls.
When these events were part of
a particularly important yearly
festival, such as the festival of
SAN GIOVANNI, workers
were able to take the day off to
celebrate them.

Balls would be held in homes with courtyards or local squares, and houses would be decorated with tapestries and specially built arches so that they looked as grand as possible. Dancers would dress up in splendid costumes and spectators would be entertained by musicians. Other entertainment for the crowd would include jugglers and **STILT WALKERS**.

The early evening would be lit up by torchlight as a procession travelled through the narrow streets. As it got darker, stunning **FIREWORKS** would be set off for the entire city to see.

CAN YOU SPOT?

- A woman holding up a gold glass
- A musician with a broken string
- Tom
- A torch that has blown out
- Digby the cat
- A juggler using fiery torches
- An animal that has joined the dancers

HOME

Tom ran up to Granny Bea and gave her a huge hug.

As he did, there was a sudden . . . **WHOOSH!**

. . . and just like that, Tom was home!

"Did you have fun, Tom?" asked Granny Bea, as Digby wriggled out of her arms and started meowing for more chicken.

"It was extraordinary!" said Tom, taking off his tunic. "I wish you could have seen everywhere I explored!"

"Oh, I think I did," Granny Bea said with a wink . . . and Digby just purred.

Can you go back and spot Granny Bea in every scene?

SOLUTIONS

MEDICI SCULPTURE GARDEN
Pages 6–7

- Tom
- A group of artists sketching a sculpture
- A gardener carrying a tree
- Digby the cat
- Children playing a game of chess
- A statue that has lost its head
- A stonemason moving some marble

PIAZZA DELLA SIGNORIA
Pages 8–9

- Someone tossing coins into the fountain
- Someone who is dropping important slips of paper from a bag
- A donkey and cart carrying supplies
- Money being exchanged
- A prisoner being taken through the square
- Tom
- Digby the cat

WEDDING PROCESSION
Pages 10–11

- A woman with a baby
- The bride's wedding chest
- Tom
- An elderly couple dancing together
- Digby the cat
- A group of musicians
- A contract of marriage

FLORENCE CATHEDRAL
Pages 12–13

- An artist painting upside down
- A group of teenagers chatting on a bench
- Tom
- A group of women praying
- A table covered in wool
- Someone about to light a candle
- Digby the cat

MICHELANGELO'S STUDIO
Pages 14–15

- Michelangelo working on a sculpture on a ladder
- A woman reading a book of poetry
- An orange sculpture that looks just like Digby
- Tom
- Carving tools on a table
- A painting of the Medici sculpture garden
- Digby the cat

PONTE VECCHIO
Pages 16–17

- Digby the cat
- Someone pouring out water and waste
- A fishmonger selling a bucket of fish
- Tom
- A woman selling tomatoes
- A donkey munching on some hay
- A dog stealing some meat

SOLUTIONS (continued)

THE ARNO RIVER
Pages 18–19

- Two children playing with dolls
- Tom
- A young boy collecting scraps of wool
- Dyed cloth being hung in a shed
- Digby the cat
- Someone who has fallen asleep in a pile of wool
- A boat with a leak

COUNTRYSIDE
Pages 20–21

- Leonardo's flying machine
- A farmer who is taking a nap
- Tom
- Leonardo doing a sketch
- A man sneakily eating some olives
- A donkey with an empty cart
- Digby the cat

COMBAT TRAINING
Pages 22–23

- Tom
- A knight whose armour is too heavy
- A condottiere signing his contract
- Digby the cat
- A crossbow that has misfired
- A child who has snuck on to a horse
- A soldier with dirty armour

FESTIVAL GAMES
Pages 24–25

- The referee shouting angrily
- An athlete who is covered in sand
- Tom
- A player who has fallen over
- Digby the cat
- The cannon used to start the match
- A rat that has snuck on to the playing field

ARTIST WORKSHOP
Pages 26–27

- Two people mixing different paint colours
- Someone getting measured for a new outfit
- An artist painting some furniture
- A family having their portrait painted
- Digby the cat
- Tom
- An artist creating copies of a painting

PALAZZO MEDICI
Pages 28–29

- Tom
- A husband and wife sharing a plate of vegetables
- A hungry dog
- Digby the cat
- A blackbird pie
- A spilled flask of wine
- A servant dropping some meat

SOLUTIONS (continued)

CARNIVAL BALL
Pages 30–31

- A woman holding up a gold glass
- A musician with a broken string
- Tom
- A torch that has blown out
- Digby the cat
- A juggler using fiery torches
- An animal that has joined the dancers

Glossary

APPRENTICE   A person who is employed and trained by an expert

ARNO RIVER   The river running through Florence that allowed products to be shipped outside the city

ARCHAEOLOGIST   Someone who studies history by digging up and examining historical objects

CACCE   Multiple points, or goals, scored in a game of calcio

CALCIO   An early form of football that was popular in Renaissance Florence

CANNON   A heavy weapon on wheels that can fire a dangerous metal ball

CASSONE   A bride's wedding chest, usually made from wood and beautifully decorated

COMMISSION   To give someone a role or responsibility, usually in return for payment

CONDOTTIERE   The leader of a group of mercenaries, hired to protect Florence

CONFRATERNITY   A group of people who come together with a purpose, such as to feed the poor

CONTRACT   An agreement that is made, between two or more people or organisations, that must be kept

CONVENT   A place where a group of nuns live together

CROSSBOW   A bow that fires metal arrow-like bolts when it is pulled back and released

DATORI INDIETRO   The four players that protect the goals in a game of calcio

DAVID   Michelangelo's giant marble sculpture of David, a Biblical figure

FIREWORK Traditionally made by burning metal powders to create white and yellow shapes in the sky

FLORENTINE A person who lives in Florence or who calls the city their home

FLYING MACHINE One of Leonardo's inventions – very impressive although it never flew

GUILD A group of employers who gather together to combine their wealth and power for a cause

KNIGHT A soldier who wears heavy armour and often fights on horseback to protect his city or country

LEONARDO DA VINCI A famous and successful painter, sculptor, scientist and inventor

MADONNA The Italian name for the Virgin Mary, an important figure in Christianity

MANNERISM An art style focused on beauty over accuracy to real-life

MEDICI The surname of a very powerful family in Renaissance Florence

MEDIEVAL The name for the period of time that came immediately before the Renaissance

MERCENARY A soldier who is paid to defend a person or place

MERCHANT Someone who sells and supplies a particular type of item

MONA LISA A famous portrait of a woman, painted by Leonardo da Vinci

PASSAGEWAY A long or narrow path that allows you to travel between two places

PATRON Someone who financially supports a person or subject – such as an artist or building

PLOUGHING To loosen or turn up soil before sowing seeds or planting

PRUNING To cut extra pieces off a plant so that it can grow better in the future

RAW WOOL Animal wool that has not had any colours or chemicals added to it

SALA A room in a home, often used for entertaining guests

SAN GIOVANNI The Italian name for Saint John, an important figure in the Christian Biblie

SCULPTURE A piece of art that is 3D, usually carved from wood or marble or made from metal or plaster

SIGNORIA The Florentine government – their job was to decide how the city should be run

STILT WALKER An entertainer who performs by balancing on high sticks, called stilts

STONEMASON A person whose job is to work with uncarved stone, such as marble

TRADE To give someone something in exchange for an item of similar value e.g. money

VILLA A type of house, often with a garden or other land attached to it

WOOL GUILD One of the most powerful Florentine guilds, run by employers from the wool industry

Index